FEEL THE BEAT

Dance Poems that Zing from Salsa to Swing

written by Marilyn Singer * illustrated by Kristi Valiant

Dial Books for Young Readers

All Over the World, Dancing Is Joy

All over the world,
dancing
is
joy.
Move your feet.
Spin.
Sway.
Just
feel the beat,
the rhythm.
Find
a partner.
Grab
your shoes.
All you can lose are
the blues.
Dance, dance away.
Now's your chance!
What do you say?

Joy Is Dancing All Over the World

What do you say?
Now's your chance.
Dance, dance away
the blues.
All you can lose are
your shoes.
Grab
a partner.
Find
the rhythm.
Feel the beat.
Just
sway,
spin,
move your feet.
Joy
is
dancing
all over the world!

Cha-Cha

Birthday.
Uncle Nate.

Good food.
Cleaned my plate.

Old songs
on CDs.

They float
on the breeze.

Here comes
my grandma.

Says let's
cha-cha-cha.

I don't
know these moves.

My feet
feel like hooves.

Oof, what
do I fix?

And then
something clicks!

Okay,
it's old school.

I say,
cha-cha's cool!

Hip-Hop

At school we brag about
what our parents do.
Some fix cars. Some fix teeth.
Some work at the zoo.
Maggie's father sells computers,
Jonah's sells shampoo.
My dad, he spins 'round on his head
with his B-Boy crew!

No fumbling, no bumbling,
my pops is tops at tumbling.
He's elastic, so fantastic.
Papa's so gymnastic!

He will swipe and windmill.
He'll slide on his knees,
do lots of flares and coin-drops.
He'll boomerang and freeze.
Everyone who's in my class
thinks that he's the bomb.
Yep, he's great, I say, but wait
until you see my mom!

Foxtrot

I can't believe
that's my sister.
She never had any grace.
Now watch her glow—
star of the show,
dressed up in lace
with a look-at-me face!

I can't believe
that's my sister.
I really hope that she wins.
Her foxtrot is fine,
so much better than mine.
I can't believe that we're twins!

Merengue

I merengue,
you merengue.
So does Cousin Marty.
All of us merengue—
when we have a party.
Moving sideways,
turning wrists,
while we do
our pretzel twists.
We sway our hips,
we shift our legs,
like we're whipping
lots of eggs.
We take a little
break and then,
we merengue
once again.

Square Dance

Got a partner, lost my shoe.
Allemande left? I haven't a clue.
Somebody tell me what to do.
I don't know how to square dance!

Did that caller give a cue?
Don't promenade me. Shoo, boy, shoo!
Maybe I'm coming down with flu.
Let me get out of square dance.

Bow to Francisco, bow to Sue.
One more swing. It's over! Whew!
I tried real hard, but alas, it's true.
I'm flunking out of square dance!

Hora

Join me, Laura!
It's the hora!
Start slow. That's fine.
Hold on, grapevine!
Circle so fast.
Puff, puff, who'll last?
Hands high, our group
moves in, yells, "Whoop!"
Hands down, we're back,
spinning 'round Zach,
high in his chair,
to show we share
his day, his joy,
bar mitzvah boy!

Samba

It's time for Carnival,
to dance and masquerade!
Coming out the door
to join the grand parade,
there's my friend Isabel
under a samba spell!

She's got a dress with fringe.
She wears a hat with fruits.
I like to watch her bounce
each time the whistle toots.
She boom-boom-booms so well
under the samba spell!

She gets to ride a float
and when she's passing by,
she blows a kiss and waves.
To think she once was shy!
She's come out of her shell
under the samba spell!

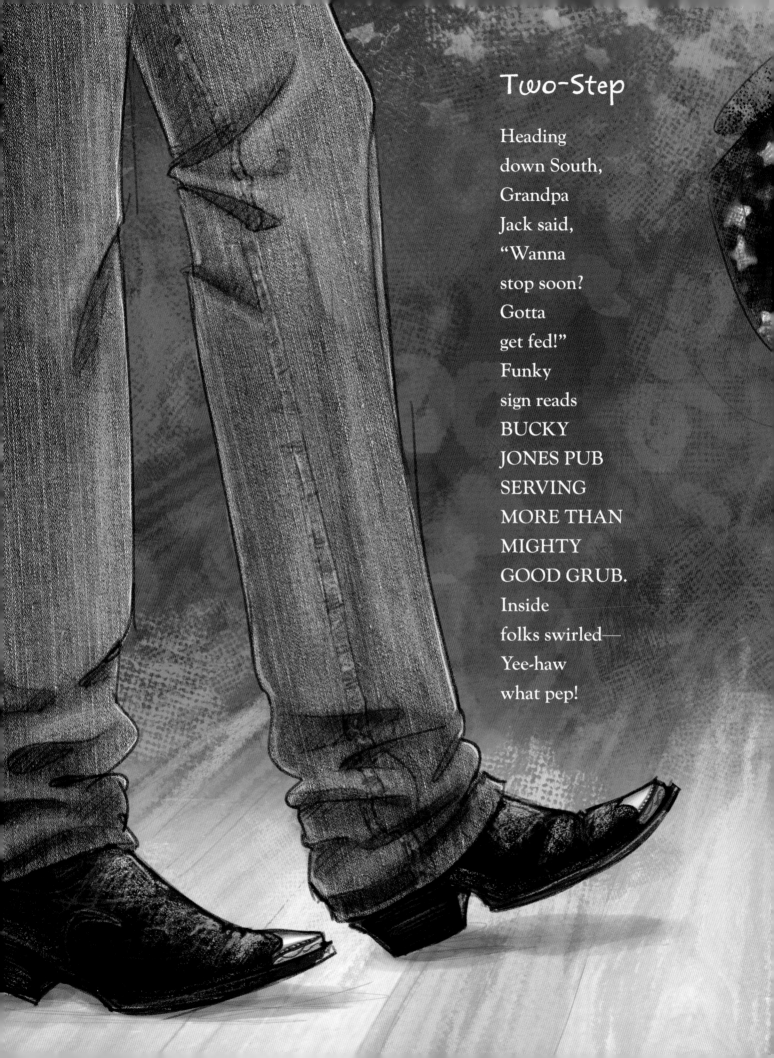

Two-Step

Heading
down South,
Grandpa
Jack said,
"Wanna
stop soon?
Gotta
get fed!"
Funky
sign reads
BUCKY
JONES PUB
SERVING
MORE THAN
MIGHTY
GOOD GRUB.
Inside
folks swirled—
Yee-haw
what pep!

Cooking
down home
Texas
two-step!
"Order
that dance!"
Grandpa
Jack hoots.
"Show off
these red
fancy-
pants boots!"
Chicken
tastes great.
So does
fried fish.
But the
two-step's
my favorite
new dish!

Salsa

Our teacher says, "First . . .

Feel the beat
      in your feet,
in your heart.
      Then you start.

Take a turn.
      Soon you'll learn
what is hot,
      what is not.

Don't be shy.
      Come on, try.
In this class,
      show some sass."

So I do.
      Take my cue,
take my chance.
      Salsa dance!

Argentine Tango

Everywhere around the world
from Hong Kong to Pago Pago,
people gather in the streets.
They do the Argentine tango.

Arianna from New York,
Armando from Durango
wonder, *Can we do these steps?*
Can we get the hang? Oh!

"Forward side, not forward back!"
Armando hollers, "Dang! No!
This is not a Texas two-step."
Ari adds, "It's no fandango.

Let's try again." And so they do.
Success, sweet as a mango!
They've got the walk, the catlike stalk,
the Argentine tango!

Conga

We're at the MALL.
I'm very BORED.
I hate the STORES,
I hate the HORDE.

"Just one more SHOP,"
my mother PLEADS.
"Just one more DRESS,"
she says she NEEDS.

"Just one more SHOP"
turns into FOUR.
I'm gonna SCREAM,
I'm gonna ROAR.

Then there's a BLAST
of music. NEAT!
Then there's a LINE
of dancers. SWEET!

Uh uh uh, KICK!
You cannot WHINE
when you are ON
a conga LINE!

Uh uh uh, KICK!
A flash mob BALL!
Keep shopping, MOM!
I love the MALL!

Waltz

Watch me pitch.
Watch me hike.
See me spin
    on my bike.
In the gym,
I do vaults.
But I'm best
    at the waltz.

In a play
I was Prince
Charming, now
    ever since
my heart does
somersaults
each time I
    hear a waltz.

Watch me call
Sis a brat,
mess my room,
    scare the cat.
Yeah, I have
lots of faults.
But no lie—
    I can waltz!

Bhangra

Sister, sister,
beautiful bride,
we dance for you.
We dance with pride.
We pump, we jump,
stamp side to side,
push hands up high
and then we cry:
Balle, balle!
Hurray, hurray!
Kick, kick, and smile
in bhangra style!

Sister, sister,
beautiful dove,
we dance for you.
We dance with love!
Balle, balle!
We shout hurray!
to celebrate
your wedding day!

Swing Dance

You can borrow books and magazines.
You can look at stuff on computer screens.
You can find out things for your next report,
get a DVD of almost any sort.

You can learn to draw, play a game like chess.
You can read to dogs. You can make a dress.
You can hear a talk, watch a puppet show.
There are lots of reasons that we go . . .

to the library,
but mom and me,
tonight we swing.
That's our new thing.
We're gonna swing.

We step . . . step . . .
rock step.
We're full . . .
of pep.
We Lindy hop.
Bibbidy-bop!
We Lindy hop!

On the plaza in July,
underneath the summer sky
where you can get to hear good bands,
kick your feet, wave your hands,
we're gonna swing.
That's our new thing.
We're gonna swing!

Today we read about finance,
looked up the capital of France.
We found a book about a pug.
But tonight we're here to jitterbug.

We'll bring it, zing it,
ring-a-ding-ding it,
do our hot new thing.
We're gonna SWING!

Polka

Polka days,
polka craze.
Oompah-pah,
squeeze box plays.

Merry din.
All my kin
sing along,
then hop in.

What a scene!
Folks careen.
Who will be
Polka Queen?

Auntie Bea?
Cousin Dee?
Holy cow!
They picked me!

I am crowned,
twirled around.
Big applause!
What a sound!

Such a blast!
Let this last.
Sigh. Oh, my,
this went fast.

Moonlight beams.
Now it seems,
time to have
polka dreams.

Notes About the Dances

Cha-Cha (aka Cha-Cha-Cha)

A playful, lively dance, originating in Cuba, that was especially popular in the 1950s and '60s. It is still fun to dance today. The name comes from the pattering of the dancers' feet and from the scraping sound of the guiro, one of the many Latin percussion instruments used to play cha-cha music. The basic cha-cha movement is made up of two slower steps and three quick ones. It starts on the second beat of a song: *TWO, three, cha-cha-cha, TWO, three, cha-cha-cha.*

Hip-Hop

A broad range of freestyle movements that began as street dances in New York City and Los Angeles and that includes breaking, popping, locking, animation, krumping, and other styles. Hip-hop is danced to a strong beat, often to rap music, and, traditionally, it is not performed to counts the way dances such as cha-cha, foxtrot, swing, and waltz are. The emphasis is on individual expression, but also "battling"—competitions between dancers.

Foxtrot

An elegant dance made famous in movie musicals in the 1930s and '40s by Fred Astaire and Ginger Rogers. It was danced to big band music, and it became one of the most popular ballroom dances of all time. Currently, it is danced with a partner both in ballroom competitions and on social occasions, such as weddings. One common foxtrot pattern is the box step of four beats, with the first and third beats held longer: *ONE, two-and, THREE, four-and, ONE, two-and, THREE, four-and.*

Merengue

A party dance from the Dominican Republic that is popular all over Latin America and the Caribbean, as well as the United States. Partners move their hips and feet sideways or while turning to fast music. The rhythm is a steady *ONE-two, ONE-two.*

Square Dance

A country dance, which grew out of folk dances such as the reel and the jig. It is performed by four couples arranged in a square, traditionally to live music played on the fiddle, banjo, and other folk instruments. A caller calls out the steps, which include *allemande, promenade,* and *swing your partner.*

Hora

A circle dance that is popular at bar mitzvahs, bat mitzvahs, weddings, and other Jewish celebrations. Dancers hold hands and step in a weaving, grapevine motion with equal beats. Then they move into the center of the circle with a loud yell. They often dance around the bar/bat mitzvah boy or girl, who is held up on a chair.

Samba

A Brazilian dance that is performed at Carnival, when people samba in colorful costumes in the street and on top of huge, fancy floats. It has a complex rhythm, featuring percussion and is often danced at a fast tempo. The basic movement is: *one a-TWO, three a-FOUR.* Social samba is danced with a partner in clubs and at parties, but Carnival samba dancers dance alone.

Two-Step

A popular country/western dance, also called the Texas Two-Step, performed in a line or with a partner. It can be danced to a variety of tempos. The basic pattern is *step-together, walk, walk (quick-quick, slow, slow).* It can start with either the quick or slow steps.

Salsa

A Latin dance that developed from Cuban and Afro-Cuban dances. The dish called salsa is a hot sauce, and the dance is a spicy blend of different styles. It features fast footwork and lots of turns. There are different styles, but the basic rhythm pattern is: *one, TWO, three . . . five, SIX, seven . . . one, TWO, three . . . five, SIX, seven . . .*

Argentine Tango

A social dance that began in Argentina and Uruguay and is now popular all over the world. Tango dance festivals—*milongas*—are often held outdoors, and they attract people of all ages. The tango is danced to a strong, repetitive rhythm and there are certain patterns of movements, such as the *ocho*, which is a figure eight. However, dancers often improvise their steps, reacting to the music and to their partners.
* A note on rhyme: Pago Pago is pronounced "pango pango," rhyming with tango.

Conga

A Cuban line dance performed at carnivals, parties, and by some flash mobs (groups of people that show up in public places to put on a surprise performance). To the beat of a strong drum rhythm, dancers hold each other's shoulders or waist and shuffle forward, then kick, alternating legs: *one, two, three, KICK!*

Waltz

A graceful, romantic ballroom dance, featuring flowing, rotating movement and smooth rise and fall on the heels and toes. It is often performed in plays and movies based on fairy tales, such as *Cinderella* and *Beauty and the Beast*. Its famous and distinct rhythm goes: ONE, *two, three,* ONE, *two, three.*

Bhangra

Originally a vigorous folk dance from the Punjab region of India and Pakistan, it has now become popular worldwide throughout South Asian communities at weddings, birthday parties, and other celebrations. Today it is often danced to a mixture of traditional music and hip-hop, both of which feature a strong drumbeat. To show happiness, dancers will shout words such as *balle balle* or *hoi hoi*—"hooray" or "yay!"

Swing Dance

A group of dances, including Lindy hop, jitterbug, jive, and Charleston, danced to jazz and popular music, featuring a lot of turns and also acrobatic lifts. It is especially known for syncopation—accenting musical beats that are not usually stressed. A typical swing pattern is: *step, step, ROCK-step (slow, slow, QUICK-quick).* Swing dance began in American Black communities in the 1920s and spread across the United States and the world. Today it is still popular among both older and younger crowds.

Polka

A Central European folk dance that is perhaps the only nineteenth-century dance still widely popular today. Polka music is played on the accordion and tuba, as well as other horns and also woodwind instruments. Famous for its "oompah-pah" rhythm, one of the simplest and best-known versions goes *"heel and toe and away we go!"*

To Laurie Shayler,
dance teacher extraordinaire
–M.S.

To my swing dancing brother, Matt.
With love,
–K.V.

Acknowledgments:

Thanks to my dance partner, Steve Aronson; to Laurie Shayler and
my other dance teachers, Jose Luis Leon and Ricardo Leon; to Brenda Bowen,
Steve Coyle, Rebecca Kai Dotlich, Cara Gargano, and Natalie Hoyle Ross; and to
Lucia Monfried and all the other good folks at Penguin.

Dial Books for Young Readers
Penguin Young Readers Group
An imprint of Penguin Random House LLC
375 Hudson Street, New York, NY 10014

Text copyright © 2017 by Marilyn Singer. Illustrations copyright © 2017 by Kristi Valiant.

Library of Congress Cataloging-in-Publication Data
Names: Singer, Marilyn, author. | Valiant, Kristi, illustrator.
Title: Feel the beat : dance poems that zing from salsa to swing / Marilyn Singer ; illustrated by Kristi Valiant.
Description: New York : Dial Books for Young Readers, [2017]
Identifiers: LCCN 2016000633 | ISBN 9780803740211 (hardcover)
Classification: LCC PS3569.I546 A6 2017 | DDC 811/.54—dc23 LC record available at http://lccn.loc.gov/2016000633

Book and CD manufactured in China

10 9 8 7 6 5 4 3 2

Designed by Jasmin Rubero
Text set in Goudy Catalogue MT ST

The art was drawn and painted in Photoshop using
a Cintiq display and pressure-sensitive pen.